Since 1888, the National Geographic Society has funded more than 12,000 research, exploration, and preservation projects around the world. The Society receives funds from National Geographic Partners, LLC, funded in part by your purchase. A portion of the proceeds from this book supports this vital work. To learn more, visit natgeo.com/info.

Printed in China
19/RRDS/1

NATIONAL GEOGRAPHIC
KiDS

PUZZLE
book of
SPACE

Tons of **COOL**
ACTIVITIES
and **FUN FACTS**

NATIONAL GEOGRAPHIC
WASHINGTON, D.C.

CONTENTS

SOLAR SYSTEM...6

INNER
SOLAR SYSTEM....8

Think you've got what it takes to tackle these stellar space puzzles? Test your talents with fun crosswords, sudoku, and more! Need a little help? No worries, you'll find solutions in the back of the book.

OUTER
SOLAR SYSTEM...28

MOONS: NATURAL SATELLITES ... 46

STARS AND CONSTELLATIONS ... 58

SPACE EXPLORATION AND HISTORY 70

SOLUTIONS ... 86

SOLAR SYSTEM

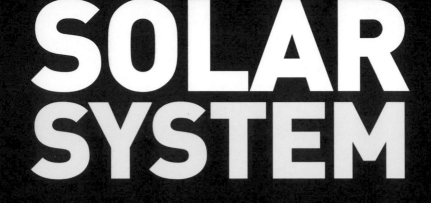

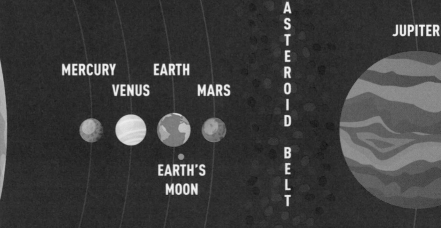

SUN

MERCURY

VENUS

EARTH

MARS

EARTH'S
MOON

ASTEROID BELT

JUPITER

Our solar system is made up of one star, which we call the sun, as well as eight planets, five dwarf planets, and many moons, asteroids, meteors, comets, and a whole lot of ice, gas, and dust—it's a very busy place!

The **FIRST FOUR PLANETS** in the solar system are known as the **INNER PLANETS**. The **FINAL FOUR** are known as the **OUTER PLANETS.**

SATURN

URANUS

NEPTUNE

K
U
I
P
E
R

B
E
L
T

INNER SOLAR SYSTEM

Read on for **FUN FACTS** and **PUZZLES** about **EARTH'S CLOSEST NEIGHBORS!**

An **ASTEROID** that hit **EARTH** around **65 MILLION YEARS AGO** is linked to the **EXTINCTION** of **DINOSAURS.**

CROSSWORDS

Fill in the crosswords by solving the cryptic clues below.

Can you work out the inner solar system code word using the letters in the shaded squares?

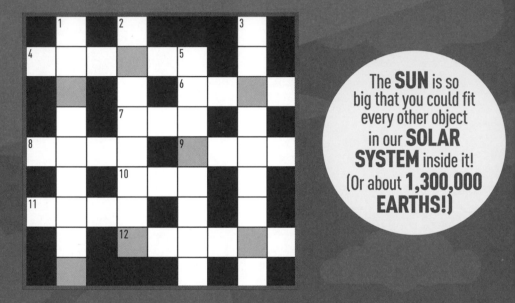

The **SUN** is so big that you could fit every other object in our **SOLAR SYSTEM** inside it! (Or about **1,300,000 EARTHS!**)

ACROSS

4 Meal eaten outdoors
6 Turn over and over
7 Organ you see with
8 Not hot
9 Additionally
10 Opposite of in
11 Assist
12 Continent where you find England and France

DOWN

1 Not trustworthy
2 You put a letter in this before mailing it
3 Device used to study stars
5 Any animal

The **SUN** is the **SCORCHING HOT STAR** of our **SOLAR SYSTEM.** Even though it is **95 MILLION MILES** (152 million km) **AWAY,** it gives us **HEAT** and **LIGHT, SUSTAINING LIFE ON EARTH.**

ACROSS

4 Asia or Europe, for example
6 Boy's name
8 Strong feeling of annoyance
9 Sweet and sticky liquid
10 Item of neckwear often worn with a suit
12 Person in a story

DOWN

1 Where you live
2 Vanish from sight
3 Heaviness
5 Number in a trio
6 Simple
7 Country whose capital is Oslo
11 Thought or suggestion

SUDOKU

Solve the sudoku to launch the spacecraft to Mercury.

Fill in the blank squares so that numbers 1 to 6 appear once in each row, column, and 3x2 box.

MERCURY is the **SMALLEST PLANET,** not much **LARGER** than our **MOON.**

2	4		3		
1	5				
4			6		3
6		5			
				2	4
				3	

MERCURY is the **CLOSEST PLANET** to the **SUN,** which makes it the **HOTTEST PLACE** to be ... right? Well, although **ONE SIDE** of **MERCURY** is **EXTREMELY HOT,** there is no atmosphere to keep the heat in. That means that the **SIDE FACING AWAY** from the sun gets **VERY COLD.**

	2		4		
			3	6	
				1	
	4				3
	1	3			
2		4	1	3	

If you were on **MERCURY**, the **SUN** would appear **THREE TIMES LARGER** in the sky than it does on **EARTH**, and a whole lot **BRIGHTER!**

WORD SEARCHES

Can you find the solar system words?

Search left to right and up and down to
find the space words listed in the boxes below.

VENUS is one of EARTH'S NEIGHBORS,
but it is very DIFFERENT FROM EARTH.
Covered in VOLCANOES and LAVA FLOWS,
VENUS is the HOTTEST PLANET in the
SOLAR SYSTEM.

asteroid

comet

gravity

light

meteoroid

moons

orbit

planets

star

sun

i	r	b	r	o	r	b	i	t	a
l	r	l	x	l	h	q	p	a	e
u	l	p	l	a	n	e	t	s	n
m	i	a	g	r	a	v	i	t	y
u	g	c	j	a	j	s	n	e	r
e	h	o	k	a	a	t	m	r	k
p	t	m	t	e	a	a	o	o	a
u	m	e	t	e	o	r	o	i	d
e	l	t	r	s	o	o	n	d	p
e	l	p	t	r	a	o	s	u	n

Ceres
craters
Earth
Mars
Mercury
rocky
solid
valleys
Venus
volcanoes

```
k  u  z  e  p  r  o  c  k  y
s  t  t  m  t  y  e  r  t  a
q  t  v  e  o  m  b  a  t  b
q  m  a  r  s  c  j  t  k  x
v  o  l  c  a  n  o  e  s  p
e  v  l  u  k  e  a  r  t  h
n  c  e  r  e  s  d  s  p  p
u  t  y  y  t  l  b  d  x  s
s  t  s  o  l  i  d  m  b  t
l  o  e  j  i  m  o  h  l  e
```

VENUS is the **BRIGHTEST OBJECT** in the **NIGHT SKY** after the **SUN** and our **MOON.**

VENUS was named after the **ROMAN GODDESS** of **LOVE** because of its brightness and beauty in the **NIGHT SKY.**

WORD JUMBLES

Return to Earth by rearranging the jumbled letters to reveal Earth-related words.

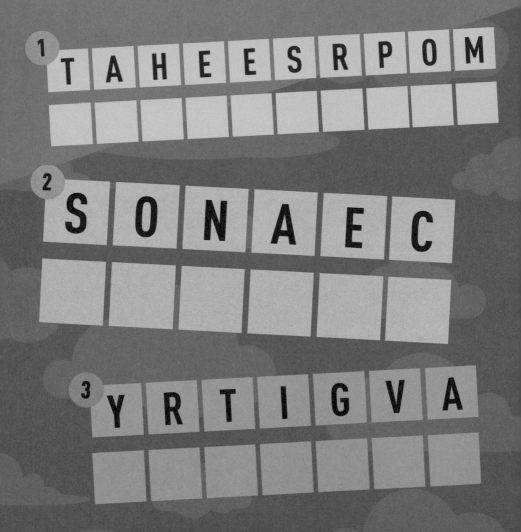

1. T A H E E S R P O M

2. S O N A E C

3. Y R T I G V A

4 M S U H N A

70 percent of **EARTH'S** surface is covered by **OCEANS.** That's a lot of **WATER!**

5 S L N A A M I

EARTH is a very special **PLANET.** It is our **HOME,** and the only planet in the universe known to **SUPPORT LIFE!** Sheltered by a **PROTECTIVE ATMOSPHERE, EARTH** is **HOME** to **TREES, PLANTS,** and **ANIMALS** that are all able to live thanks to an **ABUNDANCE OF WATER** and **BREATHABLE AIR.**

17

MAZES

Work your way around the mazes on Mars until you reach the top of Olympus Mons.

MARS is home to the tallest **MOUNTAIN** in the **SOLAR SYSTEM**, **OLYMPUS MONS,** which is **2.5** times **TALLER** than **MOUNT EVEREST, EARTH'S** highest **MOUNTAIN.** But watch out, it's a **VOLCANO,** too!

MARS is Earth's closest **NEIGHBOR.** Also called the **RED PLANET, MARS** was named after the **ROMAN GOD OF WAR** because of its blood red color. Regular **DUST STORMS** mean that the **SURFACE OF MARS** is covered in a **THICK LAYER OF RED DUST.**

WORD WHEELS

Can you unscramble the space objects in the three word wheels?

ASTEROID **FLORENCE** swept past Earth in September 2017. **ASTRONOMERS** were surprised to find that it had not one, but **TWO MOONS** in **ORBIT!**

V U
E
S N

The **PLANETS** of our solar system aren't alone in orbiting the **SUN**—they are joined by **MILLIONS** of **LUMPS** of **ROCK** that are like mini-planets. These **SPACE ROCKS** are called **ASTEROIDS.** The **ASTEROID BELT** is a huge concentration of them in **ORBIT** between **MARS** and **JUPITER, SEPARATING** the **INNER** and **OUTER PLANETS.**

CODE WORDS

Can you crack these super-tricky code words? Each letter of the alphabet is represented by a number. Some have been given to start you off. Fill in each grid with words and, once it is full, see if you can work out the code word using the letters in the shaded squares.

3	12	19	3	13		14	3	22	11	3	6	7
6		8		21		16			3		5	
3		14		20		15		15	5	13	18	3
13	3	25	20	26	12	8	15		19		5	
22		20		5		5		9	16	12	12	23
3	6	7	8	13	3	12	23		17			3
7		3		26			14		9		14
8			5		5	26	14	7	13	5	15	7
15	21	3	2	14		12		13		6		3
	5		2		2	5	11	8	12	8	5	13
18	8	10	3	6		4		24		7		19
	24		15			3		3		16		5
1	20	8	7	7	3	13		14	16	13	13	23

1	2	3	4	5	6	7	8	9	10	11	12	13
Q		E		A			I	J	X			R

14	15	16	17	18	19	20	21	22	23	24	25	26
			W	V	D			G				

CERES was considered a **COMET** when first **DISCOVERED** in **1801.** It was upgraded to a **PLANET,** but then reclassified as an **ASTEROID** until 2006, when it was classified as a **DWARF PLANET.**

1	2	3	4	5	6	7	8	9	10	11	12	13
				Q	E	V			K		H	J

14	15	16	17	18	19	20	21	22	23	24	25	26
G	A					L				R	Z	

CERES is the **LARGEST** object in the **ASTEROID BELT,** measuring about **600 MILES** (966 km) in **DIAMETER.** Because of its size, **GRAVITY** has **ROUNDED IT** into a **SPHERE.** That's one reason it's classified as a **DWARF PLANET.**

23

MATCH GAME

Match the mind-boggling magnifications below to the named pictures on the right-hand page.

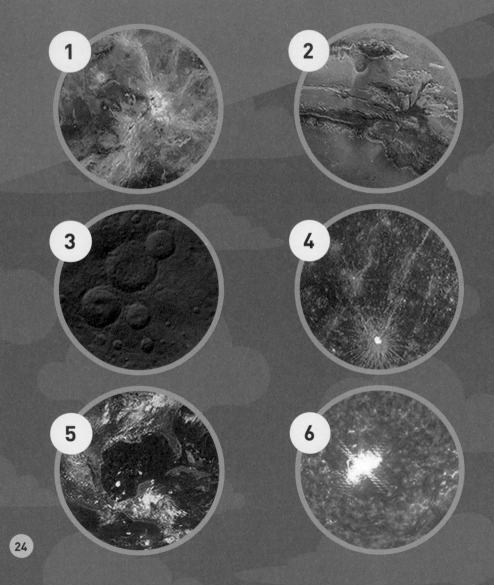

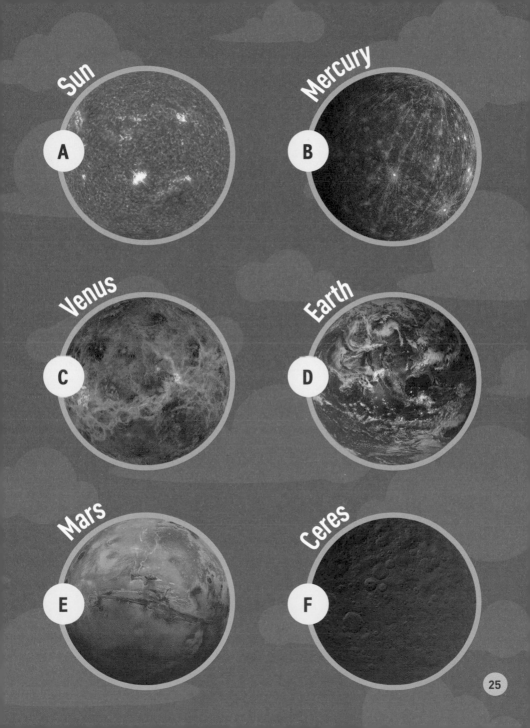

Sun
A

Mercury
B

Venus
C

Earth
D

Mars
E

Ceres
F

25

QUIZ WHIZ

Do you know the answers to the inner solar system questions below?

1. How many inner planets are there?
   a. 1
   b. 4
   c. 8

2. The asteroid belt is found beyond the orbit of which planet?
   a. Mercury
   b. Earth
   c. Mars

3. Which is the smallest planet in the solar system?
   a. Mercury
   b. Earth
   c. Jupiter

4. Which is the only planet known to have life?
   a. Earth
   b. Venus
   c. Saturn

5. What is the largest object in the asteroid belt?
   a. Ceres
   b. Series
   c. Sirius

6. Who is the planet Mars named after?
   a. The Roman god of love
   b. The Roman god of peace
   c. The Roman god of war

7. How long is a year on Mercury?
   a. 11 Earth days
   b. 88 Earth days
   c. 888 Earth days

8. How many moons does Venus have?
   a. 0
   b. 2
   c. 4

9. What is the name of the third planet from the sun?
   a. Earth
   b. Mars
   c. Jupiter

10. Mars has a mountain that rises 16 miles (25 km) above the surrounding land. What is it called?
    a. Olympus Mens
    b. Olympus Mons
    c. Olympus Mans

OUTER SOLAR SYSTEM

Discover **FUN FACTS** and **PUZZLES** about some **FAR-OUT PLANETS.**

SATURN'S RINGS
extend **175,000 MILES** (282,000 km) out into space and are **33 to 98 FEET** (10–30 m) **THICK.**

CROSSWORDS

Launch a mission to Jupiter by cracking the cryptic clues below.

Can you work out the outer solar system code word using the letters in the shaded squares?

JUPITER has an area called the **GREAT RED SPOT,** which is thought to be a gigantic **STORM** that has been raging for at least **150 YEARS!**

ACROSS
1. Draw special attention to; best part
5. Put briefly into liquid
7. African country
8. On the ___ : about to happen
11. Large flightless Australian bird
12. Exploding star

DOWN
1. Small mammals with spiny coats
2. Spaces
3. Female child
4. Large, hairy spider
6. Surprise greatly
9. Sloping surface
10. *Finding* ___ : film about a clownfish

JUPITER is also known as the **GIANT PLANET.** Why? Because it's the **BIGGEST PLANET** in the **SOLAR SYSTEM,** at more than **300 TIMES** the **SIZE** of **EARTH!** As if that wasn't impressive enough, **JUPITER** also has the **MOST MOONS** of any planet in our solar system, with at least **67 DISCOVERED SO FAR.**

ACROSS

1 Crisis
5 Animal with a snout
7 Put an idea forward for consideration
8 Math or English, for example
11 Primary color
12 Very

DOWN

1 Opposite of cheap
2 Chickens lay these
3 Pleasant
4 The day before today
6 Have the same opinion; concur
9 Type of shoe
10 Oak or sycamore, for example

SUDOKU

Solve the sudoku to launch the spacecraft to Saturn.

Fill in the blank squares so that numbers 1 to 6 appear once in each row, column, and 3x2 box.

4			5		
	6		2		
		4			6
5		6			
		2		1	
		3			5

SATURN has **SEVEN GROUPS** of **RINGS,** which orbit at different speeds. They are made of **BILLIONS** of **PIECES** of **ICE** and **ROCK** that range in size from as small as **DUST PARTICLES** to as huge as **MOUNTAINS!**

				6	4
					5
	4		1		
		3		2	
6					
3	1	5	6		2

SATURN'S DAYS are less than **HALF** as long as Earth's: only **10 HOURS** and **14 MINUTES.** But its **YEARS** are more than **29 TIMES LONGER.**

WORD SEARCHES

Can you find the outer solar system words?

Search left to right and up and down to find the space words listed in the boxes below.

The icy giant **URANUS** is very **COLD** and **WINDY.** Also called the **SIDEWAYS PLANET,** it appears to be **ROLLING AROUND** the **SUN** on its **SIDE.** This **UNUSUAL ANGLE** means that the **SEASONS ON URANUS ARE EXTREME,** with **HALF OF THE PLANET** being plunged into a **DARK WINTER** for **21 YEARS** at a time.

cold
gas giants
huge
Jupiter
moons
Neptune
red spot
rings
Saturn
Uranus

q	m	h	o	s	s	u	s	g	u
i	o	u	j	r	a	r	e	w	w
l	o	g	u	k	t	a	r	t	k
q	n	e	p	t	u	n	e	i	g
t	s	r	i	l	r	u	d	u	s
o	n	i	t	l	n	s	s	u	e
s	r	n	e	w	p	e	p	n	t
z	f	g	r	p	p	c	o	l	d
g	a	s	g	i	a	n	t	s	n
o	r	y	e	x	s	i	z	r	i

These are names of some of the moons in the outer solar system! Can you find them all?

Charon
Hyperion
Iapetus
Mimas
Miranda
Phoebe
Thebe
Titania

w	p	s	i	a	p	e	t	u	s
r	p	e	c	a	t	h	e	b	e
z	l	s	h	b	r	y	b	t	j
p	b	c	a	i	s	p	u	i	p
h	y	d	r	o	g	e	n	t	l
o	p	j	o	o	m	r	o	a	u
e	b	q	n	l	i	i	o	n	t
b	f	s	l	r	m	o	b	i	o
e	z	m	i	r	a	n	d	a	o
l	v	w	e	k	s	v	u	l	f

SCIENTISTS believe that deep within their atmospheres, **URANUS** and **NEPTUNE** rain **DIAMONDS!**

◀ URANUS

35

MAZES

Work your way around these mesmerizing mazes until you reach the exit!

NEPTUNE is the **PLANET FARTHEST FROM THE SUN,** our solar system's only source of heat and light, so it is also the **DARKEST** and **COLDEST PLANET** in the **SOLAR SYSTEM.**

NEPTUNE has an average **TEMPERATURE** of **−353°F** (−214°C) on its **SURFACE** but is **12,600°F** (7000°C) at its **CORE.**

WORD JUMBLES

Send a spacecraft to Pluto by rearranging the jumbled letters to reveal space-related words.

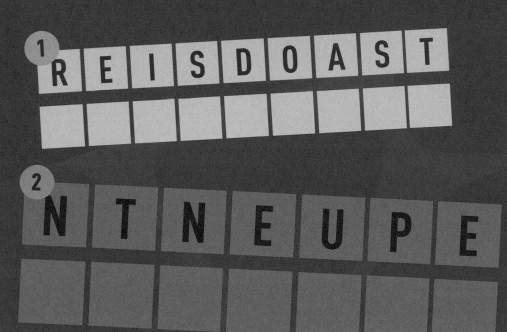

1 R E I S D O A S T

2 N T N E U P E

3 U S A N R U

4 R A D W F

PLUTO is so far away from the sun that its orbit takes a very long time—**ONE YEAR** on **PLUTO** is about as long as **248 YEARS** on **EARTH!**

5 T E I R U P J

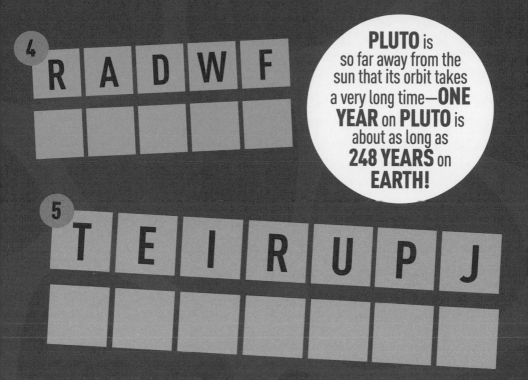

For a long time, **PLUTO** was considered the **NINTH PLANET** of our **SOLAR SYSTEM**, but in **2006** it was **RECLASSIFIED** as a **DWARF PLANET. PLUTO** is usually **COVERED IN ICE**, but for some parts of its orbit the **ICE MELTS** a little and forms a thin **NITROGEN ATMOSPHERE.**

CODE WORDS

Can you crack these super-tricky code words? Each letter of the alphabet is represented by a number. Some have been given to start you off. Fill in each grid with words and, once it is full, see if you can work out the code word using the letters in the shaded squares.

> **OBJECTS** in the **KUIPER BELT** are thought to be **LEFTOVER PIECES** from the beginning of our **SOLAR SYSTEM.**

Letter/number key:

1	2	3	4	5	6	7	8	9	10	11	12	13
P		G	D	H		A			T	R		

14	15	16	17	18	19	20	21	22	23	24	25	26
E							V		Y			C

▼ ERIS

The **KUIPER BELT** is a concentration of **MILLIONS** of **ROCKY, ICY OBJECTS** that orbit our sun beyond the orbit of **NEPTUNE.** These objects may **HOLD CLUES** about the **ORIGINS OF** our **SOLAR SYSTEM,** but they are so far away that they are **VERY DIFFICULT FOR ASTRONOMERS TO STUDY.**

1	2	3	4	5	6	7	8	9	10	11	12	13
E						T		L		H		D

14	15	16	17	18	19	20	21	22	23	24	25	26
		S					Q		F		A	P

41

MATCH GAME

Match the mind-boggling magnifications below to the named pictures on the right-hand page.

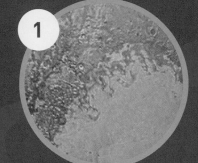

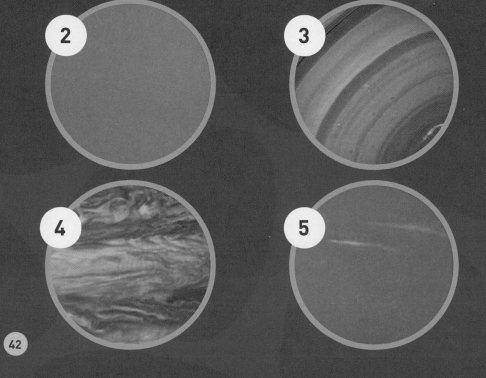

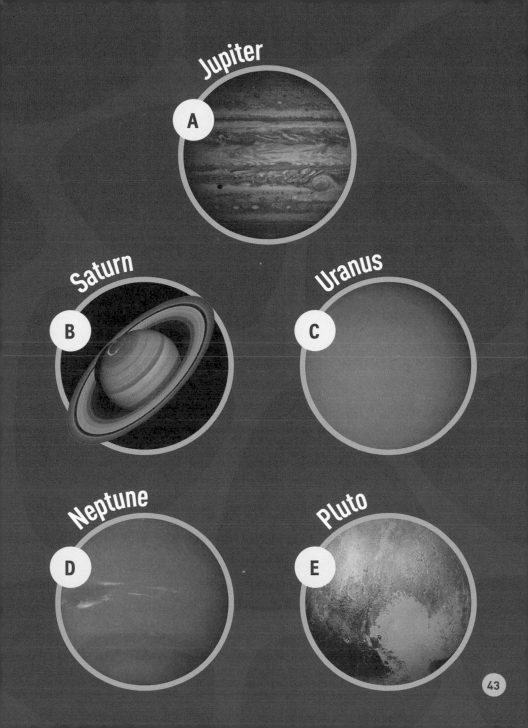

Jupiter

A

Saturn

B

Uranus

C

Neptune

D

Pluto

E

43

WORD WHEELS

Can you unscramble the planets
in the three word wheels?

QUIZ WHIZ

Do you know the answers to the outer solar system questions below?

1. What are Jupiter and Saturn sometimes known as?
   a. Rock giants
   b. Gas giants
   c. Liquid giants

2. Which is the second largest planet?
   a. Saturn
   b. Neptune
   c. Venus

3. Which of these is a famous feature of Jupiter?
   a. Great Green Spot
   b. Great Blue Spot
   c. Great Red Spot

4. How many moons does Jupiter have?
   a. Less than 20
   b. Less than 40
   c. More than 60

5. One of Jupiter's moons is the largest in the solar system. What is it called?
   a. Thebe
   b. Callisto
   c. Ganymede

6. What is Saturn mainly made of?
   a. Lithium
   b. Hydrogen
   c. Carbon

7. What is the name of Saturn's largest moon, which is the only moon known to have a dense atmosphere?
   a. Phoebe
   b. Titan
   c. Mimas

8. What is the name of the seventh planet from the sun?
   a. Uranus
   b. Pluto
   c. Mars

9. Who is the planet Neptune named after?
   a. The Roman god of the sea
   b. The Roman god of lightning
   c. The Roman god of destiny

10. Which of these is known as a dwarf planet?
    a. Pluto
    b. Mercury
    c. Earth

MOONS: NATURAL SATELLITES

Learn about marvelous moons with **FUN FACTS** and **PUZZLES** in this chapter.

CALLISTO, one of **SATURN'S MOONS**, is the **MOST CRATERED** object in the solar system.

CROSSWORDS

Crack the crosswords to land safely on the moon by solving the cryptic clues below.

Can you work out the moon code word using the letters in the shaded squares?

The first person to set foot on the **MOON** was **NEIL ARMSTRONG,** in **1969.** He famously said, "That's one small step for man, one giant leap for mankind."

ACROSS
1 Day before Thursday
4 Help and assist
6 Item blown by a referee
9 Appliance
10 Exciting trip

DOWN
1 Opposite of east
2 Make something longer by pulling it
3 One trip around the sun
5 Exclusive
7 U.S. space agency
8 Where you are right now

LUNA, CYNTHIA, SELENE—there are many names for our **MOON,** but whatever you want to call it, there's no denying that it's **EARTH'S CLOSEST COMPANION** within the solar system. As **EARTH** orbits the sun, the **MOON COMES WITH US,** orbiting our planet at the same time.

Earth's **MOON** is the **ONLY OTHER PLACE** in the **SOLAR SYSTEM THAT HUMANS HAVE VISITED,** so far ...

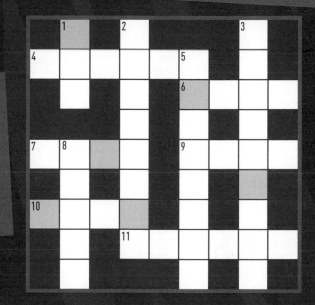

ACROSS

4. Way of doing something
6. You use these to hear
7. Fix; repair
9. Talk to your friends
10. Border
11. No person

DOWN

1. You do this with a needle and thread
2. Kids
3. Orange spread
5. Give details about
8. Someone older than you

EARTH'S ▶ MOON

SUDOKU

Solve the sudoku to launch the test flight to Phobos.

Fill in the blank squares so that numbers 1 to 6 appear once in each row, column, and 3x2 box.

The moons of **MARS,** called **PHOBOS** and **DEIMOS,** are among the **SMALLEST MOONS** in the **SOLAR SYSTEM.** Like Earth's moon, both have **LUMPY, DUSTY SURFACES** covered in **CRATERS.**

	4				
	2		4	3	
	3				5
1					
2	6	5		1	4
				2	

Both **PHOBOS** and **DEIMOS** orbit quite close to the **MARTIAN SURFACE**, so if you were to **STAND ON ONE**, Mars would take up a **LOT** of the **SKY VIEW**.

6			5	2	
	6			5	
	3			4	
	1	4			3
	2				

◄ DEIMOS

▼ PHOBOS

SCIENTISTS think that in the future, one of **MARS'S** moons could be used as a **BASE** for **ASTRONAUTS** while they **OBSERVE** the **RED PLANET.**

WORD SEARCHES

Can you find the moon-related words?

Search left to right and up and down to find the space words listed in the boxes below.

JUPITER is the **BIGGEST PLANET** and also has the **BIGGEST MOON—GANYMEDE,** which is nearly **TWICE THE SIZE** of **EARTH'S MOON!**

One of **JUPITER'S MOONS,** called **Io,** is home to over **400** active **VOLCANOES,** which makes it the most active object in the entire **SOLAR SYSTEM!**

atmosphere

core

crust

eclipse

full moon

mantle

mountains

new moon

oceans

water

f	f	n	y	l	t	o	p	o	a
a	u	e	s	p	c	o	r	e	t
r	l	w	c	j	w	c	z	l	m
s	l	m	r	j	a	e	s	e	o
u	m	o	u	n	t	a	i	n	s
g	o	o	s	s	e	n	u	p	p
a	o	n	t	a	r	s	g	g	h
t	n	t	e	c	l	i	p	s	e
q	i	s	a	s	r	d	y	j	r
u	y	y	a	m	a	n	t	l	e

These are names of some of the moons in the solar system! Can you find them all?

Ariel
Callisto
Charon
Europa
Ganymede
moon
Oberon
Rhea
Titan
Triton

u	t	s	w	j	m	o	o	n	v
r	h	e	a	d	e	n	b	d	u
m	a	u	w	i	t	o	e	a	d
a	b	r	a	c	h	a	r	o	n
e	r	o	u	e	v	d	o	f	a
u	y	p	t	i	t	a	n	r	r
d	c	a	l	l	i	s	t	o	i
s	s	g	a	n	y	m	e	d	e
r	b	b	t	r	i	t	o	n	l
n	r	i	w	s	x	q	i	t	r

◄ CALLISTO

▼ GANYMEDE

▼ EUROPA

53

MAZES

Work your way around these mesmerizing mazes until you reach the exit!

▼ PHOEBE

PHOEBE orbits **SATURN** in the **OPPOSITE DIRECTION** of most of the planet's other **MOONS.**

SATURN has at least **62 MOONS** in its **ORBIT,** and they are all very different from one another.

HYPERION ▶

▼ TITAN

TITAN, Saturn's largest moon, is **MADE UP OF NITROGEN** and appears bright orange in color. **HYPERION,** one of Saturn's smaller moons, **HAS A LUMPY SHAPE**—like a rocky potato!

WORD WHEELS

Can you unscramble the moons
in the three word wheels?

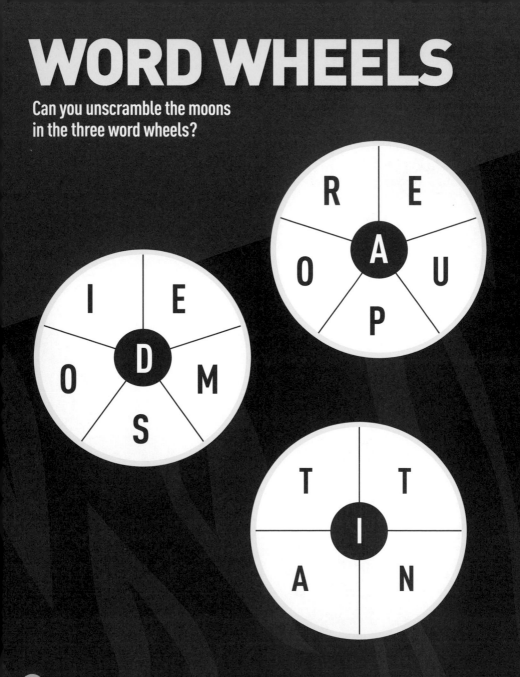

QUIZ WHIZ

Do you know the answers to the moon questions below?

1. How many moons does the planet Mars have?
   a. 0
   b. 2
   c. 4

2. How long ago is Earth's moon thought to have formed?
   a. About 4.5 million years ago
   b. About 45 million years ago
   c. About 4.5 billion years ago

3. How long does it take for the moon to orbit Earth?
   a. About 17 days
   b. About 27 days
   c. About 37 days

4. With more than 400 active volcanoes, which moon of Jupiter is the most geologically active object in the solar system?
   a. Io
   b. Jo
   c. Mo

5. Which of these is a moon of Jupiter?
   a. Europa
   b. Phobos
   c. Helene

6. Which is Saturn's second largest moon?
   a. Rhea
   b. Lea
   c. Shea

7. Saturn's moon Mimas has a distinctive feature that has a diameter almost one third of Mimas's diameter. What is it?
   a. A giant impact crater
   b. A giant lake
   c. A giant alien spaceship

8. Titania is the largest moon of which planet?
   a. Pluto
   b. Uranus
   c. Saturn

9. How many known moons does the planet Neptune have?
   a. 0
   b. 14
   c. 74

10. Which of these statements about Charon, the largest moon of Pluto, is true?
    a. It is very large in comparison to the size of Pluto.
    b. It is actually bigger than Pluto.
    c. It is the smallest known moon in the solar system.

STARS AND CONSTELLATIONS

Read on for **FUN FACTS** and **PUZZLES** all about **STARS.**

No one knows who **FIRST CHARTED** the **CONSTELLATIONS**, but it is thought to have been the **SUMERIANS** or **BABYLONIANS, 4,000 YEARS AGO!**

CROSSWORDS

Fill in the puzzle using the cryptic clues to the right.

Can you work out the stars and constellations code word using the letters in the shaded squares?

The constellations we know will look very different **100,000 YEARS** from now. Because of how we move through space, **SCIENTISTS** predict that one day the **BIG DIPPER** will look more like a **BIG DUCK!**

▼ BIG DIPPER

You may have heard of the **BIG DIPPER,** also known as the **PLOUGH,** but did you know that it belongs to a larger constellation? It forms part of **URSA MAJOR,** commonly known as the **GREAT BEAR.** The handle of the Big Dipper represents the bear's tail—even though bears don't really have tails!

ACROSS

4. Dad
6. Want what someone else has
7. Zeus and Ares are these
8. Opposite of home
9. An edible seed
10. Split into smaller parts

DOWN

1. The night of October 31st
2. Ten times one hundred
3. Exposed or uncovered
5. A sister or uncle, for instance

ACROSS

1. Opposite of public
6. Building designer
8. A legendary story, usually for children
9. Not fortunate

DOWN

2. Comes after a wedding
3. Place with rides and fun things to do
4. Capital city of Wales
5. Tool used to attach pieces of paper together
7. Country where one finds Rome

SUDOKU

Solve the sudoku to make Polaris sparkle.

Fill in the blank squares so that numbers 1 to 6 appear once in each row, column, and 3x2 box.

LITTLE DIPPER ▶

URSA MINOR is another name for the constellation known as the **LITTLE BEAR.** Just as the Big Dipper forms the Great Bear's tail, the **LITTLE DIPPER** forms the **LITTLE BEAR'S TAIL!** The brightest star in **URSA MINOR** is **POLARIS,** Earth's north celestial pole.

Top puzzle:

		6		4	
	3				
			3	5	
3	2	5			4
				1	
	6		4		

Bottom puzzle:

			3		
2	3	5	4		1
1					
					2
		2	6	1	
		3			

WORD SEARCHES

Can you find the star-related words?

Search left to right and up and down to find the star words listed in the boxes below.

heat
light
Orion
Pegasus
Perseus
Pisces
Sirius
sunspot
Taurus
Ursa Major

i	x	t	u	l	i	g	h	t	u
a	h	f	s	b	j	h	b	z	r
p	a	u	u	t	a	u	r	u	s
r	p	a	n	n	r	o	g	c	a
p	e	r	s	e	u	s	a	j	m
i	g	h	p	r	c	s	k	t	a
s	a	e	o	r	i	o	n	k	j
c	s	a	t	t	r	i	w	g	o
e	u	t	k	c	t	u	t	x	r
s	s	i	r	i	u	s	i	h	a

SIRIUS is the **BRIGHTEST STAR** in the **NIGHT SKY,** which is why its name comes from a Greek word meaning "glowing" or "scorching." It is also known as the **DOG STAR,** because it forms part of **CANIS MAJOR—** a constellation that is said to look like a large dog.

These are names of some stars and constellations in the sky.
Can you find them all?

Andromeda
Aries
Auriga
Betelgeuse
Cygnus
Draco
Gemini
Hercules
Sagitta
Ursa Minor

l	a	a	u	s	m	l	u	b	s
z	a	r	i	e	s	e	r	e	a
h	e	r	c	u	l	e	s	t	n
s	s	a	g	i	t	t	a	e	d
d	m	u	e	s	e	t	m	l	r
r	o	r	m	i	o	p	i	g	o
a	c	i	i	q	b	i	n	e	m
c	y	g	n	u	s	r	o	u	e
o	a	a	i	y	g	o	r	s	d
i	i	t	t	i	l	a	t	e	a

SIRIUS is so far away, it takes EIGHT YEARS for LIGHT FROM the STAR TO REACH US.

◄ CANIS MAJOR

MAZES

Journey through these mesmerizing mazes until you reach the exit!

ORION is a CONSTELLATION known by many cultures around the world and has a lot of DIFFERENT MYTHS associated with it. ORION'S brightest STARS are RIGEL, which looks like one star from Earth but is actually made up of a number of stars, and BETELGEUSE, which is a red supergiant.

◄ORION

WORD WHEELS

Can you unscramble the star words
in the three word wheels?

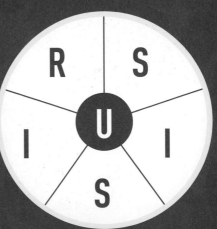

QUIZ WHIZ

Do you know the answers to the stars and constellations questions below?

1. What is the name of the star closest to our planet?
   a. Vega
   b. Sun
   c. Procyon

2. A star shines by fusing hydrogen into which other element in its core?
   a. Copper
   b. Gold
   c. Helium

3. When a massive star collapses at the end of its life cycle, it might form which of these?
   a. Yellow hole
   b. Blue hole
   c. Black hole

4. What is the name of the brightest star in the night sky?
   a. Sirius
   b. Aquarius
   c. Serious

5. What is the name of the second brightest star in the night sky?
   a. Octopus
   b. Tinopus
   c. Canopus

6. Rigel is the brightest star in which constellation?
   a. Onion
   b. Ocean
   c. Orion

7. Which of these is the name of a constellation?
   a. Andromeda
   b. Butdromeda
   c. Alsodromeda

8. What is another name for the constellation Ursa Major?
   a. Great Chair
   b. Great Bear
   c. Great Stair

9. What name is given to a famous pattern formed by seven bright stars in Ursa Major?
   a. The Brow
   b. The Plough
   c. The Cow

10. Leo is a constellation. Its name is Latin for:
    a. Lion
    b. Tiger
    c. Bear

SPACE EXPLORATION AND HISTORY

Ready to learn about **SPACE EXPLORATION?**
Read on for **FUN FACTS** and **PUZZLES.**

The **HUBBLE SPACE TELESCOPE** has captured a photo that peers **12.2 BILLION YEARS** into the universe's past.

TIMELINE OF EXPLORATION

For decades, humans have been trying to find out more about what goes on in our solar system. Astronauts, space shuttles, and artificial satellites are just a few of the ways people have explored outer space.

Check out the timeline below for major milestones.

▲
SPUTNIK 1

1957 TO 1969

1957 The first artificial satellite, Sputnik 1, launched

1959 First photograph of Earth from orbit

1961 First man in space

1963 First woman in space

1965 First images of Mars

1965 First space walk

1966 First spacecraft to land on the moon

1969 Man lands on the moon

1970 TO 1979

1970 First lunar rover

1971 First space station

1972 Apollo 17 lands on the moon.

1973 First images of Jupiter

1974 First images of Venus

1977 Voyager spacecraft launched

1979 First images of Saturn

1980 TO 1989

1980 Voyager 1 passes Saturn

1981 First space shuttle launch

1986 Space shuttle *Challenger* disaster

1986 Voyager 2 passes Uranus

1989 Voyager 2 passes Neptune

HUBBLE
SPACE TELESCOPE ▶

SATURN ▶

2000 TO PRESENT

2000 First orbit of an asteroid

2001 First landing on an asteroid

2001 First tourist in space

2004 First orbit of Saturn

2011 Final space shuttle launch

2016 Astronomers present models suggesting a new planet exists in the outer solar system

1990 TO 1999

1990 Magellan arrives at Venus

1990 Hubble Space Telescope launched

1991 First asteroid flyby

1995 First orbit of Jupiter

1997 First Mars rover

1998 First module of International Space Station launched

MARS
ROVER ▶

CROSSWORDS

Help the astronauts crack these cryptic crosswords.

Can you work out the space exploration code word using the letters in the shaded squares?

The first two dogs to make a **RETURN FLIGHT** from **SPACE** were Belka and Strelka—they were in space for a day in **1960** before safely returning to **EARTH.**

ACROSS

1 Country where you find New York
6 Amuse
8 Time when you are young
9 Greeting to a guest

DOWN

2 A two-wheeled vehicle with an engine
3 Place in a school where lessons take place
4 Bird with impressive tail feathers
5 Contain as part of a whole
7 Circular

An **ASTRONAUT** is a **PERSON** who **TRAVELS INTO SPACE.**
The **FIRST PERSON IN SPACE** was **YURI GAGARIN,**
a Russian astronaut who made a 108-minute spaceflight in 1961.
VALENTINA TERESHKOVA was the **FIRST WOMAN IN SPACE.**
In 1963, she spent three days there, orbiting Earth 48 times!

ACROSS
1 Related to the eye
6 Bitter-tasting substances
7 Your way of writing your name
8 A sound you make when surprised

DOWN
1 Completely different things
2 Symbol in an alphabet
3 Free time
4 In great need
5 A dog's tail when happy

SUDOKU

Solve the sudoku to launch the space shuttle.

Fill in the blank squares so that numbers 1 to 6 appear once in each row, column, and 3x2 box.

1	5				
3				4	
		6		2	
	3			6	
	2				3
				1	6

The first **SPACE SHUTTLE LAUNCH** in **1981** was the beginning of a new era for **SPACE TRAVEL.** Space shuttles **TOOK OFF LIKE ROCKETS,** but **LANDED LIKE PLANES,** so they were much more reusable than other kinds of rockets.

Up to six people can **LIVE** in the **INTERNATIONAL SPACE STATION.**

In 1998, the **INTERNATIONAL SPACE STATION** was launched into orbit around Earth. It is as **BIG** as a **SIX-BEDROOM HOUSE,** has two bathrooms, many science labs, and even a **GYM!**

2			1		4
		1			5
				1	
	6				2
4			2		3
3		5			1

WORD SEARCHES

Can you find the space-related words?

Search left to right and up and down to find the space words listed in the boxes below.

s	p	a	c	e	w	a	l	k	x
a	s	t	r	o	n	a	u	t	a
t	e	e	l	h	u	b	b	l	e
e	a	r	b	o	k	o	r	s	x
l	u	n	a	r	r	o	v	e	r
l	r	g	a	l	a	x	y	a	n
i	v	o	y	a	g	e	r	p	p
t	f	u	s	h	u	t	t	l	e
e	m	i	l	k	y	w	a	y	p
s	p	a	c	e	s	u	i	t	h

VOYAGER 1 ▲

astronaut

galaxy

Hubble

lunar rover

Milky Way

satellites

shuttle

space suit

space walk

Voyager

SATELLITES are used to **OBSERVE PLANETS** from **ORBIT.** They don't need to land, so they can **EXPLORE PLANETS** that are very far away, like **URANUS** and **NEPTUNE.**

In **2012**, a **SPACECRAFT** called **VOYAGER 1** officially became the first human-made **OBJECT** to **LEAVE** our **SOLAR SYSTEM**.

```
f  l  y  b  y  s  o  y  m  j
a  q  s  u  l  c  t  y  o  o
h  m  o  d  u  l  e  z  o  g
a  m  a  g  e  l  l  a  n  o
p  p  h  i  l  a  e  u  f  q
o  j  q  c  a  s  s  i  n  i
l  w  n  b  i  e  c  s  e  v
l  m  a  r  s  r  o  v  e  r
o  s  x  a  g  s  p  j  l  u
e  g  a  l  i  l  e  o  t  v
```

ROVERS are special **ROBOTIC VEHICLES** designed to **EXPLORE** the **SURFACES** of other **PLANETS**. They don't need to have people in them, so they can go to faraway places like **MARS**.

Apollo
Cassini
flyby
Galileo
Magellan

Mars rover
module
moon
Philae
telescope

▼ ROVER

VOYAGER 1 is now in interstellar space, over **13,048,795,037 MILES** (21,000,000,000 km) from **EARTH**—and still going!

SPOT THE DIFFERENCE

Compare the two images of the astronaut. Can you spot the five differences between the images?

MATCH GAME

Match the mind-boggling magnifications below
to the named pictures on the right-hand page.

1

2

3

4

5

6

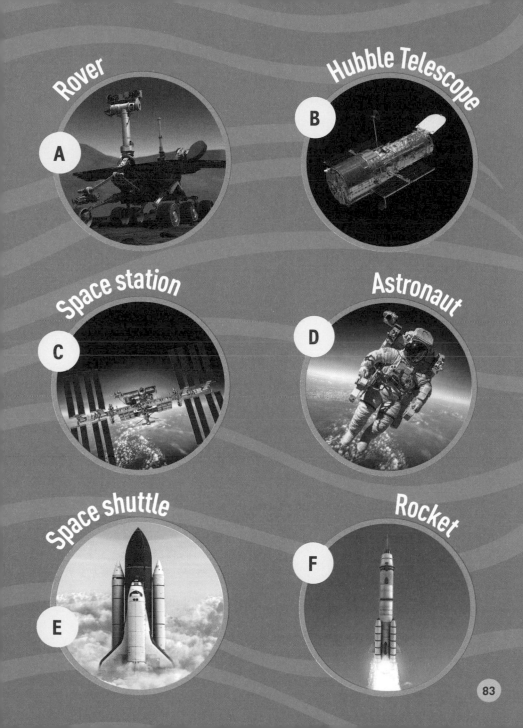

Rover

A

Hubble Telescope

B

Space station

C

Astronaut

D

Space shuttle

E

Rocket

F

83

WORD WHEELS

Can you unscramble the space exploration words in the three word wheels?

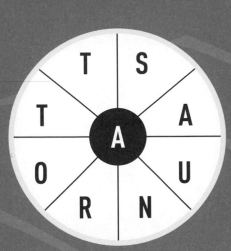

QUIZ WHIZ

Do you know the answers to the space exploration questions below?

1. Who is famously associated with the telescope?
   a. Galileo
   b. Euclid
   c. Socrates

2. Which of these is the name of a famous telescope?
   a. Bubble Space Telescope
   b. Hubble Space Telescope
   c. Rubble Space Telescope

3. What was the first planet discovered through a telescope?
   a. Jupiter
   b. Saturn
   c. Uranus

4. In which year did humans first land on the moon?
   a. 1949
   b. 1969
   c. 1989

5. What was the name of the first artificial satellite launched?
   a. Spacenik 1
   b. Robotnik 1
   c. Sputnik 1

6. What is the name of a person who goes into space?
   a. Braveonaut
   b. Staronaut
   c. Astronaut

7. Who was the first person to walk on the moon?
   a. Neil Aldrin
   b. Neil Collins
   c. Neil Armstrong

8. What is the name of the artificial satellite in low Earth orbit that is visited by astronauts?
   a. Multinational Space Station
   b. Supernational Space Station
   c. International Space Station

9. Which of these is the name of a rover exploring Mars?
   a. Curiosity
   b. Boredom
   c. Indifference

10. Which hugely successful space mission to Saturn ended in September 2017 with the probe intentionally destroying itself?
   a. Mir
   b. Skylab
   c. Cassini

SOLUTIONS

CROSSWORDS 10–11

Code word: **PLANETS**

Code word: **MERCURY**

SUDOKU 12–13

2	4	6	3	1	5
1	5	3	4	6	2
4	1	2	6	5	3
6	3	5	2	4	1
3	6	1	5	2	4
5	2	4	1	3	6

3	2	6	4	5	1
4	5	1	3	6	2
6	3	2	5	1	4
1	4	5	6	2	3
5	1	3	2	4	6
2	6	4	1	3	5

WORD SEARCHES 14–15

WORD JUMBLES 16–17

1 – Atmosphere   3 – Gravity   5 – Animals
2 – Oceans   4 – Humans

MAZES 18–19

WORD WHEELS 20–21

Venus   Mercury   Asteroid

CODE WORDS 22–23

Code words:
ASTEROID
BELT

Code word :
EARTH

MATCH GAME 24–25

1 – C Venus   3 – F Ceres   5 – D Earth

2 – E Mars   4 – B Mercury   6 – A Sun

QUIZ WHIZ 26

1. b – 4   6. c – The Roman god of war

2. c – Mars   7. b – 88 Earth days

3. a – Mercury   8. a – 0

4. a – Earth   9. a – Earth

5. a – Ceres   10. b – Olympus Mons

SOLUTIONS

CROSSWORDS 30–31

Code word: SATURN

Code word: JUPITER

SUDOKU 32–33

4	2	1	5	6	3
3	6	5	2	4	1
2	3	4	1	5	6
5	1	6	4	3	2
6	5	2	3	1	4
1	4	3	6	2	5

5	3	1	2	6	4
4	6	2	3	1	5
2	4	6	1	5	3
1	5	3	4	2	6
6	2	4	5	3	1
3	1	5	6	4	2

WORD SEARCHES 34–35

MAZES 36–37

WORD JUMBLES 38–39

1 – Asteroids   3 – Uranus   5 – Jupiter

2 – Neptune   4 – Dwarf

CODE WORDS 40–41

Code words:
**KUIPER
BELT**

Code word:
NEPTUNE

MATCH GAME 42–43

1 – E Pluto   3 – B Saturn   5 – D Neptune

2 – C Uranus   4 – A Jupiter

WORD WHEELS 44

Neptune   Jupiter   Saturn

QUIZ WHIZ 45

1. b – Gas giants
2. a – Saturn
3. c – Great Red Spot
4. c – More than 60
5. c – Ganymede
6. b – Hydrogen
7. b – Titan
8. a – Uranus
9. a – The Roman god of the sea
10. a – Pluto

SOLUTIONS

CROSSWORDS

Crossword 48:

```
W E D N E S D A Y
E           T     E
S U P P O R T     A R
T     R     E         R
    W H I S T L E
N       V     C       H
A     M A C H I N E
S           T         R
A D V E N T U R E
```

Code word: CRATER

Crossword 49:

```
    S   C             M
M E T H O D           A
    W   I       E A R S   R
            S           M
M E N D         C H A T   L
    L   R       R         A
E D G E         I         D
    E       N O B O D Y
R                   E     E
```

Code word: SELENE

SUDOKU 50–51

3	4	1	6	5	2
5	2	6	4	3	1
6	3	2	1	4	5
1	5	4	2	6	3
2	6	5	3	1	4
4	1	3	5	2	6

1	5	2	6	3	4
6	4	3	5	2	1
4	6	1	3	5	2
2	3	5	1	4	6
5	1	4	2	6	3
3	2	6	4	1	5

WORD SEARCHES 52–53

```
f f n y l t o p o a
a u e s p c o r e t
r l w c j w c z l m
s l m r j a e s e o
u m o u n t a i n s
g o o s s e n u p p
a o n t a r s g g h
t n t e c l i p s e
q i s a s r d y j r
u y y a m a n t l e
```

```
u t s w j m o o n v
r h e a d e n b d u
m a u w i t o e a d
a b r a c h a r o n
e r o u e v d o f a
u y p t i t a n r r
d c a l l i s t o i
s s g a n y m e d e
r b b t r i t o n l
n r i w s x q i t r
```

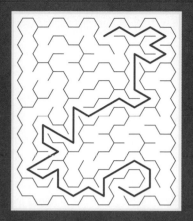

WORD WHEELS 56

Europa   Deimos   Titan

QUIZ WHIZ 57

1. b – 2
2. c – About 4.5 billion years ago
3. b – About 27 days
4. a – Io
5. a – Europa
6. a – Rhea
7. a – A giant impact crater
8. b – Uranus
9. b – 14
10. a – It is very large in comparison to the size of Pluto.

SOLUTIONS

CROSSWORDS 60–61

Code word:
LIGHT

Code word:
POLARIS

SUDOKU 62–63

2	1	6	5	4	3
5	3	4	6	2	1
6	4	1	3	5	2
3	2	5	1	6	4
4	5	3	2	1	6
1	6	2	4	3	5

4	6	1	3	2	5
2	3	5	4	6	1
1	2	4	5	3	6
3	5	6	1	4	2
5	4	2	6	1	3
6	1	3	2	5	4

WORD SEARCHES 64–65

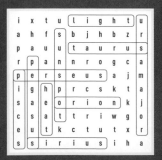

SOLUTIONS

CROSSWORDS 74–75

Crossword 1:
```
  A M E R I C A     C
P   O       L     I
E N T E R T A I N   N
A   O   O   S     C
C   R   U   S     L
O   B   N   R     U
C H I L D H O O D   D
K   K       O     E
  W E L C O M E
```

Code word: **ASTRONAUT**

Crossword 2:
```
O P T I C A L     D
P         H   E   E
P   W     A C I D S
O   A     R   S   P
S I G N A T U R E   E
I   G     C   R   R
T   I     E     E A
E   N     E       T
S         G A R B   E
```

Code word: **TELESCOPE**

SUDOKU 76–77

Sudoku 1:
1	5	4	6	3	2
3	6	2	5	4	1
4	1	6	3	2	5
2	3	5	1	6	4
6	2	1	4	5	3
5	4	3	2	1	6

Sudoku 2:
2	5	3	1	6	4
6	4	1	3	2	5
5	3	2	4	1	6
1	6	4	5	3	2
4	1	6	2	5	3
3	2	5	6	4	1

WORD SEARCHES 78–79

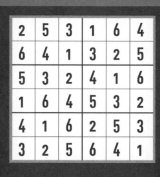

Word search 1:
```
s p a c e w a l k x
a s t r o n a u t a
t e e l h u b b l e
e a r b o k o r s x
l u n a r r o v e r
l r g a l a x y a n
i v o y a g e r p p
t f u s h u t t l e
e m i l k y w a y p
s p a c e s u i t h
```

Word search 2:
```
f l y b y s o y m j
a q s u l c t y o o
h m o d u l e z o g
a m a g e l l a n o
p h i l a e u f q
o j q c a s s i n i
l w n b i e c s e v
l m a r s r o v e r
o s x a g s p j l u
e g a l i l e o t v
```

94

SPOT THE DIFFERENCE 80–81

MATCH GAME 82–83

1 – E Space shuttle   3 – C Space station   5 – A Rover
2 – D Astronaut   4 – F Rocket   6 – B Hubble Telescope

WORD WHEELS 84

Rover   Astronaut   Telescope

QUIZ WHIZ 85

1. a – Galileo
2. b – Hubble Space
    Telescope
3. c – Uranus
4. b – 1969
5. c – Sputnik 1
6. c – Astronaut
7. c – Neil Armstrong
8. c – International Space
    Station
9. a – Curiosity
10. c – Cassini

Find the
ANSWERS!

Still seeing stars? Want to discover more about the universe? This amazing atlas is filled with fun facts, maps, games, and activities all about space travel, our solar system, outer space, and beyond!